Praise for

Good Things, Emotional Healing Journal
ADDICTION

"I recommend this workbook because I believe the path outlined in this text will work effectively, especially if it is discussed with a sponsor or an addiction specialist. It would be a wonderful adjunct to anyone's treatment who wants to attain lasting recovery."

— **Dr. Arthur P. Ciaramicoli**, author of
Performance Addiction and *Curse of the Capable*

"Good Things, Emotional Healing Journal—Addiction, is a wonderful aide in managing impulsive behaviors and in healing the suffering that accompanies them. I highly recommend this workbook because it is both inspirational and practical. It engages the reader in self-exploration while helping him or her move forward with positive attitudinal and behavioral changes. I am always searching for useful self-growth tools for my clients. This journal is one of the best!"

— **Marcia Conley**, M.A., LPC, BCIA, Psychotherapist for 40 years

"Congratulations! You are about to embark on a wondrous and difficult journey. Use this journal as your GPS. It can guide you all the way to joyous freedom. Through its simplicity and thoroughness it is an empowering aide to recovery."

— **Barbara Varney**, recovered addict, sponsor for
Marijuana Anonymous and speaker for National Alliance for the Mentally Ill

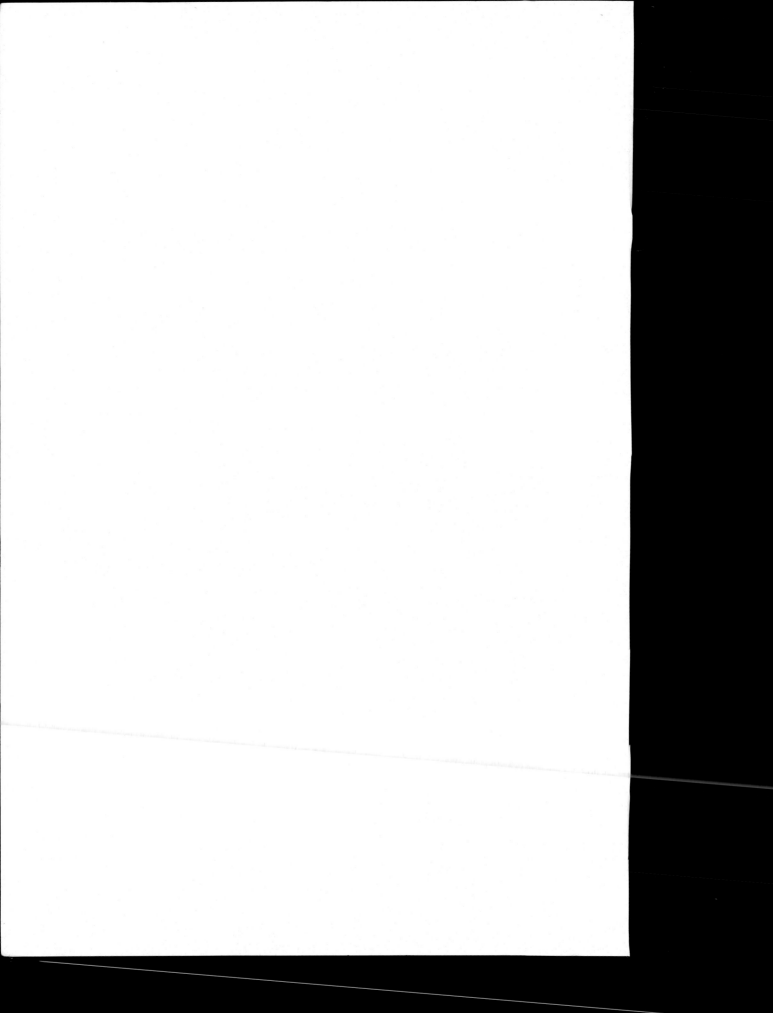

Good Things
Emotional Healing Journal

ADDICTION

EFFECTIVE STRATEGIES to MANAGE
Unwanted Habits AND Compulsive Behaviors

ELISABETH DAVIES, M.C.
Illustrated by BRYAN MARSHALL

NEW YORK

Good Things Emotional Healing Journal
ADDICTION

EFFECTIVE STRATEGIES TO MANAGE
Unwanted Habits AND Compulsive Behaviors

by ELISABETH DAVIES, M.C.
Illustrated by BRYAN MARSHALL

ISBN 978-1-61448-010-5 Paperback
ISBN 978-1-61448-011-2 eBook
Library of Congress Control Number: 2011927221

Published by:
MORGAN JAMES PUBLISHING
The Entrepreneurial Publisher
5 Penn Plaza, 23rd Floor
New York City, New York 10001
(212) 655-5470 Office
(516) 908-4496 Fax
www.MorganJamesPublishing.com

Interior Design by:
Bonnie Bushman
bbushman@bresnan.net

For all the addicts who struggle with relapse. May you know that you have value, regardless of your addiction. Never allow your addiction to stop you from sharing your inherent talents and abilities to bless others.

Acknowledgements

I would like to thank my editor Echo Surina at Philanthropology for all her insightful, professional feedback and support in making Good Things Emotional Healing Journal—Addiction a polished book.

I am very thankful to my illustrator, Bryan Marshall ("The Chosen One"), for his wonderful, audacious talent of artistically capturing addiction. His illustrations are what complete my vision for this book.

I am grateful to David Hancock, Chief Evangelist for The Entrepreneurial Author, for all his positive encouragement and insightful guidance in supporting me as a first-time author.

I want to thank all of my clients who struggle with addiction, for sharing their experiences and needs for recovery. This wealth of knowledge is what helped me confidently pass on the effective strategies in this book.

I am so appreciative of my husband, Stacy, who is always willing to help me whenever my computer does not cooperate while writing! His constant support is such a reassurance in my life.

I would especially like to thank God whose guidance is what made writing this book possible. I am in awe of the people He led me to and the wide-open path He created for me. All of this has made my journey to becoming a writer an honor.

Foreword

As a journalist I have had the opportunity to speak with people in the public eye who have struggled with addiction or helped those struggling.

In an interview I did with Dr. Drew Pinsky, host of VH1's "Sober House" and "Celebrity Rehab," he described addiction as follows; "I contemplate addiction as anybody with a family history who is developing consequences from their relationship with a substance. It's the loss of control. It's a biological disorder with a genetic base. The hallmark being the progressive use or preoccupation in the face of adverse consequence and then denial. So it's a spectrum disorder from predisposed to incipient to mild to moderate to severe."

Christopher Kennedy Lawford, nephew of President John F. Kennedy has written two books on addiction, "Symptoms of Withdrawal: A Memoir of Snapshots and Redemption" and "Moments of Clarity; Voices from the Front Line of Addiction and Recovery."

I was fortunate enough to interview him twice on the subject. Here is what he said about his addiction. "I was somebody who, and like a lot of people in "Moments of Clarity," I did not like my life. I did not like who I was. I did not like what I was doing. I did not like turning my back on the opportunities I was given. But I was powerless at the time to do anything about it." That is until he had his moment of clarity and knew he wanted to end the cycle of self –destruction.

Once you begin the process of healing or simply exploring the possibility your actions may be the result of addictive behavior, a book like this one by Elisabeth Davies can be a lifesaver. Finding professional help, adding structure and routine to diminish the cravings and staying focused on your goal will take you where you want to go and this book will help enforce the positive each step of the way.

Good Things, Emotional Healing Journal—Addiction, is interactive. You read, you think, you write and if you are honest with yourself between these pages you may just find the freedom you deserve, the freedom to live with control over impulse.

—**Patricia Sheridan**, Associate Editor/Features Pittsburgh Post-Gazette

Contents

Acknowledgements..vii

Foreword...ix

Preface 1

INTRODUCTION: You Are Not Alone In Your Addiction 5

CHAPTER 1   5 Factors That Can Increase Your Risk Of Becoming Addicted 11

CHAPTER 2   Symptoms of Addiction 15

CHAPTER 3   Some Common Addictions...19

CHAPTER 4   Addiction Inventory..21

CHAPTER 5   Effective Strategies for Managing Addiction 23

CHAPTER 6   Effective Strategy # 1: Commit To Stopping Your Addiction Now 25

CHAPTER 7   Effective Strategy #2: Visualize yourself without the addiction. 29

CHAPTER 8   Effective Strategy #3: Delay Giving In To Your Habit 33

CHAPTER 9   Effective Strategy #4: Have An Anchor 41

CHAPTER 10   Effective Strategy #5: Soothe Your Moods And Emotions 45

CHAPTER 11   Effective Strategy #6: Take Care Of Your Body....................51

CHAPTER 12   Effective Strategy #7: Pace Yourself! 57

CHAPTER 13   Effective Strategy #8: Seek Counseling With An Addiction Specialist...........63

CHAPTER 14   Effective Strategy #9: Develop An Effective Relapse Prevention Plan 69

CHAPTER 15   What are the Twelve Steps?...71

CHAPTER 16   Effective Strategy #10: Serve Others Instead Of Yourself 77

CHAPTER 17   Effective Strategy #11: Keep Your Thoughts In The Now 85

CHAPTER 18   Effective Strategy #12: Believe In Yourself 89

CHAPTER 19   Effective Strategy #13: Connect With Other People 95

CHAPTER 20   Effective Strategy #14: Sacrifice Your Addiction.........................101

CHAPTER 21   Effective Strategy #15: Strengthen Your Internal Boundaries
To Contain Uncomfortable Feelings...107

About the Author 117

About the Illustrator...117

Good Things Emotional Healing Journals COMING SOON 119

Appendix..121

Resources...123

References..125

Preface

I am really excited to be addressing the topic of addiction. It's something I know well. I too have been on addiction's deceiving, out-of-control ride with several of my own past addictions: food, cigarettes, drugs, love and work. I am also living proof—after going through years of personal counseling, continuing education, support groups, dialogue with other addicts, and a strong foundation in God that impulsive behavior and addictive symptoms can be healed and managed!

After 20 years of counseling thousands of clients, many of whom have struggled with their own impulsive habits and addictions, I've decided to share some of the most effective healing strategies I've seen help so many people like you. It is an honor to pass along these tools for a better life to you today.

Physical and emotional stress can make millions of people vulnerable to use mood-altering substances and unhealthy habits as an attempt to cope. *Good Things, Emotional Healing Journal—Addiction,* offers effective strategies and insights to manage unwanted habits and compulsive behaviors, so that you can choose healthier ways to cope with life. This user-friendly workbook offers empowering strategies, writing opportunities and addiction inventories that are all geared to assist you in healing and managing unwanted impulsive habits and addictive symptoms.

To get the most benefit from this journal I suggest you practice one effective strategy at a time and answer each question following the strategy until you can incorporate the strategy into your daily routine.

This journal is a resource that can be used throughout your life whenever you get unwanted desires or cravings or want to prevent a relapse into a past impulsive habit. Continued reinforcement of these strategies will promote longer periods of recovery and fewer relapses.

Feel free to share what you learn here with others who also want to get through life's challenging obstacles using healthy skills instead of unhealthy vices.

Because…everyone deserves to live life fully and freely!

— **Elisabeth Davies**, MC

GOOD THINGS, EMOTIONAL HEALING JOURNAL

This journal belongs to_____ _____

Some of the things I hope to accomplish as I work through this journal are...

_____

_____

_____

_____

_____

_____

_____

_____

_____

_____

_____

_____

_____

_____

_____

_____

_____

_____

_____

_____

I Can Be Addiction Free!

You Are Not Alone In Your Addiction

Addiction is an epidemic that impacts more than 140 million adults in the US.(1) In fact, the No. 1 addiction in America is food! More than 50 percent of American adolescents and adults were obese from impulsively overeating in 2007.(2)

Yet, it is the addiction that the least amount of people seek treatment for.

The second most common addiction in America is nicotine. More than 43 million Americans reported smoking cigarettes and being addicted to nicotine in 2007.(3)

The third most popular addiction in America is alcohol. Yet, it is the number one addiction that people seek treatment for. A survey done in 2007 by the National Institute of Alcohol Abuse and Alcoholism reports that 17 million Americans have alcohol disorders.(4)

Marijuana is the most commonly used illegal drug in America, with more than 16 million reported users.(5) I would like to know how many people used marijuana and didn't report it!

Work addiction is also quite common in America. Approximately 63 percent of American employees work more than 40 hours per week, and 40 percent exceed 50 hours per week.(6)

It's relatively easy to become addicted to spending. If we don't have money to spend, we can always charge it. The average American adult owns nine credit cards and has an estimated $8,000 of credit card debt.(7) In 2009, 1.4 million people filed for bankruptcy due to overspending.

Children have addictions, too. American children spent nearly 55 hours per week watching television, texting and playing video games in 2010.(8)

Two newer addictions that are quite common now are Internet surfing and gaming. These can distract us for hours.

Whenever we continue participating with a substance or habit, despite the negative consequences it causes in our life, we may be addicted.

What Is Addiction?

Addiction was defined as a disease in 1956 by the American Medical Association.(9) Addiction is a physical, chemical process. A chemical called dopamine gets released in our brain when we participate in something we find pleasurable, such as eating, bonding or sex. Our brain remembers this pleasure and wants more.

How Do We Become Addicted?

An addiction can be formed by continued participation with the substance or activity that activates the dopamine reward system in the brain. This continued participation can alter brain chemistry, causing cravings long after the substance or habit has been stopped. The cravings cause vulnerability to relapse. Relapse is a return to the substance or habit to relieve uncomfortable withdrawal symptoms.(10)

Participation with a substance or activity is often used as a form of self-medication, to calm and soothe our moods, or distract us during stressful situations or emotional difficulties.

What Is At The Root Of Addictive Disorders?

- Inability to calm, soothe or self-regulate our emotions.
- Low self-esteem and feelings of inadequacy.
- Distorted beliefs, like; 'we are not the master of our own fate' or 'control lies outside of us.'
- Inability to deeply connect in our relationships with others and God.
- Chemical imbalances caused by the body not receiving or absorbing the proper nutrients.(11)

Why Do We Stay Addicted?

- Denial that we have a problem.
- Giving in to cravings.
- Believing that our addiction is a coping mechanism.
- Caring more about self-gratification, than how our choices affect others.
- Lack of commitment to stopping the addiction.

How Can We Heal From Addictive Behavior?

- Correct our distorted beliefs, so we feel powerful in creating our future.
- Unconditionally love ourselves so we make choices that are for our highest good.
- Develop spiritual qualities to enhance our relationships and support system.
- Become skllled at managing and expressing our emotions in healthy ways.
- Get professional help for our chemical imbalances.

Addiction is treatable.

Addiction Journal

Is there anything you do habitually that is not for your highest good? What is it?

_____
_____
_____
_____
_____
_____
_____
_____
_____
_____
_____
_____
_____
_____

Have you experienced any negative consequences from participating in your habit or addictive behavior? What were the consequences?

_____
_____
_____
_____
_____
_____
_____
_____
_____
_____
_____
_____
_____
_____
_____
_____

Has anyone who knows you ever said they are concerned by your participation with your addiction/
habit? Who was concerned? What did they say?

_____

_____

_____

_____

_____

_____

_____

_____

_____

_____

_____

_____

_____

_____

_____

How did you respond to their concern? Did it make you think differently about your participation
with your addiction/habit? Why?

_____

_____

_____

_____

_____

_____

_____

_____

_____

_____

_____

_____

_____

_____

Have you ever been concerned about the amount of time you spend participating with an unhealthy habit or substance? Explain.

Have you ever switched to a different habit/addiction or increased the amount of an old habit/addiction because you weren't getting the same high stimulus as when you first started participating with it? Describe a time(s) when you did this.

_____

_____

_____

_____

_____

_____

_____

_____

_____

_____

_____

_____

_____

_____

_____

_____

_____

_____

_____

_____

_____

_____

_____

_____

_____

_____

_____

_____

_____

_____

_____

_____

_____

5 Factors That Can Increase Your Risk Of Becoming Addicted

1) Genetics

We have about a 50 percent to 60 percent chance of becoming addicted, if our parents or family members have an addiction.(12)

2) Emotions

If we have a mental health disorder that indicates a lack of self-control such as, intermittent explosive disorder, a mood disorder, untreated attention deficit or hyperactivity disorders, or if we break the law, this puts us at a greater risk of making impulsive choices, which is a quality of addiction.

There is a link between using an addiction to self medicate symptoms of depression or anxiety.(13)

Having low self-esteem increases our chances for self-destructive choices like addiction, due to not making self-care a priority.

3) Environment

If we grew up in a home with abuse, neglect or trauma, or felt unloved by our caretakers, we are at a significantly higher risk for addiction.

There is a link between food addiction (compulsive over eating) and children growing up in homes with a rejecting or non-soothing parent, due to our self-regulation mechanism, gone haywire.(10)

High-conflict relationships with parents, partners, children, peers or others also put us at a greater risk to medicate with addictive habits or substances to block out problems and manage stress.

If we grew up in an unsafe community, a midst war, violence or high crime, we are likely to have left over trauma, causing high physical and emotional stress. This leaves us at risk to seek relief with alcohol or mind-altering substances.

If we are experiencing high stress life situations, such as divorce, death of a loved one, loss of a job, financial hopelessness or any difficult life transition, this will put us at a higher risk to seek relief or distraction through a pleasure producing substance or activity.

4) Physical health

If we have any disabilities, chronic illnesses or chronic pain, this can put us at a higher risk to medicate with an addictive pain relieving substance.

If we don't accept our body shape and size, this could trigger compulsive addictive behaviors with food or exercise.

5) Spiritual life

If we were raised in a cult or philosophy with extreme views or rules, this puts us at risk to have extreme 'all or nothing' thinking, which is a quality of addiction. Feeling unfulfilled or lacking direction in life puts us at risk to medicate or distract from feeling disconnected from our meaningful purpose.

Addiction Journal

Do any of the five risk factors apply to you? Which ones?

_____

_____

_____

_____

_____

_____

_____

_____

_____

_____

_____

_____

_____

_____

_____

_____

_____

_____

Addiction,
You drown my dreams and distract me from
My fears.
Are you friend or foe?
Both faces to me you show.
So viciously you pursue me,
Making my mind a quagmire of disquiet.
Weakening my will to do what is right.
I am once again lured by your overtaking.
You are a gray mist between GOD and me.
A pestilent problem, of which I want to be free.
Addiction, hard it is to endure you.

Addiction Journal

What risk factor(s) do you try to cope with by using an unhealthy habit or substance?

_____
_____
_____
_____
_____
_____
_____
_____
_____
_____
_____
_____
_____
_____
_____
_____
_____
_____
_____
_____
_____
_____
_____
_____
_____
_____
_____
_____
_____
_____
_____
_____
_____

CHAPTER 2
Symptoms of Addiction

If you answer true to any of the following symptoms, you may have an addiction:

I do not think I have a problem, even when others tell me they are concerned about my participation with my habit and /or substance use.

True   **False**

I neglect my responsibilities and don't follow through with what I say I'm going to do, so I can participate with my habit or substance. I make excuses for my behaviors and choices.

True   **False**

I am dishonest with others and myself about how much I participate with my substance or habit. I am sneaky and manipulative to get my way.

True   **False**

I participate with my substance or habit to emotionally detach from myself and /or others. I prefer being with people who also participate with my substance or habit.

True   **False**

I am unsympathetic to how my words and choices affect others. I use relationships to benefit my own needs.

True   **False**

I have impulsive thoughts that are followed by compulsive behaviors. I don't feel in control of my will to make the right choice. I feel dependent on my habit and or substance.

True   **False**

I seek out substances and high-risk activities to feel good.

True   **False**

My personality and mood change when I participate with the addictive substance and or habit.

True   **False**

I have low self-esteem and I don't take good care of myself. I choose things that are not in my best interest.

True   **False**

My tolerance to the addictive substance or habit increases over time. I have to do more of it to get the same initial results.

True   **False**

I have negative consequences in my personal life. My relationships, job, home, legal and or financial situations are not optimal, due to my participation with my habit and/or substance.

True   **False**

Addiction Journal

Have you experienced any of the symptoms of addiction? Which ones?

_____

_____

_____

_____

_____

_____

_____

_____

_____

_____

_____

_____

Are there any symptoms you are motivated to change? Which ones? Why?

_____

_____

_____

_____

_____

_____

_____

_____

_____

_____

_____

_____

_____

_____

_____

_____

CHAPTER 3

Some Common Addictions

Drugs	Work	Relationships
Gambling	Nicotine	I.V.
Shopping/over spending	Food	Religion
Alcohol	Internet	Sports
Sex or pornography	Caffeine	Exercise
Prescription medication	Cell phone/texting	Video games

Have you participated in any of the above? Which ones?

_____

_____

_____

_____

_____

_____

_____

_____

_____

Have any of the above caused negative consequences for you? Which ones?

_____

_____

_____

_____

_____

_____

_____

_____

_____

Addiction Journal

What pleasurable habit or substance do you have difficulty doing in moderation?

CHAPTER 4

Addiction Inventory

How do I know if I'm addicted?

Take this inventory to gauge your current addictive symptoms.

Directions: Mark the box that most applies.

0=never / 1=hardly ever / 2=sometimes / 3=often / 4=usually

Addictive Symptoms	0	1	2	3	4
Compulsive: Impulsive thoughts and behaviors. "All or Nothing" thinking. Lack of moderation.					
Denial: Rationalize and minimize how often I participate with my habits. Dishonest with others. Defensive if confronted.					
Low Self-esteem: Self-critical. Allow others to devalue me. Feelings of guilt and shame. Make choices that are not in my best interest.					
Blame: Don't take ownership or responsibility for the way my life is. I make excuses and justify my behavior.					
Self-Centered: Inconsiderate of how my words and actions affect others. My wants and needs come first. Undependable					
Mood Changes: Irritable. Unpredictable and immature responses. Isolative or reclusive.					
Life Consequences: Negative outcomes from habits. Loss of job, relationships, money, etc. Lack spiritual connection or inner peace.					

Score 1-7 points Non-addictive personality traits	Score 8-14 points Mild addictive traits	Score 15-21 points Moderate addictive traits (seek treatment).	Score 22-28 points Severe addictive traits (seek treatment).

Write down the addictive symptoms from the Addiction Inventory that you marked as 2 (Sometimes) 3 (Often) or 4 (Usually) in.

_____

_____

_____

_____

_____

_____

_____

_____

Pick one of the addictive symptoms that you wrote down above.

The strategies that will help you manage each symptom, are listed on page 23. Practice one effective strategy at a time and complete the questions and exercises that go with each strategy, until you can lower your score to a 1 (Hardly ever), or a 0 (Never) on the Addiction Inventory.

Do this with each category written above until you score a 1 or 0 on the addiction inventory.

Example

If you marked a 2 (Sometimes) 3 (Often) or 4 (Usually) on the addictive symptom 'Low Self-esteem,' start on strategy #5 on page 45.

When you have finished, work on strategy #6 on page 51.

When you have finished, do strategy #7 on page 57.

After you complete that, work on strategy #12 on page 89.

Then complete strategy #15 on page 107.

Keep working on these strategies, at your own pace until you can lower your score to a 1 or a 0.

Then start with the next symptom you marked a 2, 3, or 4 in, on the Addiction Inventory.

CHAPTER 5

Effective Strategies for Managing Addiction

Symptom Strategies to help you manage symptoms

Compulsive:	*Strategy #3* *Page 33*	Strategy #4 *Page 41*	Strategy #5 *Page 45*	Strategy #7 *Page 57*	Strategy #11 *Page 85*
Denial:	*Strategy #1* *Page 25*	*Strategy # 8* *Page 63*	*Strategy # 9* *Page 69*	*Strategy # 11* *Page 85*	*Strategy # 14* *Page 101*
Low Self-esteem	*Strategy # 5* *Page 45*	*Strategy # 6* *Page 51*	*Strategy # 7* *Page 57*	*Strategy # 12* *Page 89*	*Strategy #15* *Page 107*
Blame	*Strategy #1* *Page 25*	Strategy # 8 *Page 63*	Strategy #9 *Page 69*	Strategy # 14 *Page 101*	
Self-centered	*Strategy #5* *Page 45*	*Strategy # 8* *Page 63*	*Strategy # 10* *Page 77*	*Strategy # 13* *Page 95*	
Mood Changes	*Strategy # 4* *Page 41*	*Strategy # 5* *Page 45*	*Strategy # 7* *Page 57*	*Strategy # 8* *Page 63*	*Strategy # 11* *Page 85*
Life Consequences	*Strategy # 1* *Page 25*	*Strategy # 2* *Page 29*	*Strategy # 8* *Page 63*	Strategy # 9 *Page 69*	Strategy # 14 *Page 101*

CHAPTER 6

Effective Strategy # 1

Commit To Stopping Your Addiction Now

Having a strong desire to stop your impulsive habit will bring forth the motivation needed to do the work required to change your behavior. Telling yourself you will quit tomorrow or next week, proves that you are not truly committed yet. Commit to stopping each moment you realize you are participating in your habit. This will help get you back on track quicker and shorten your relapses.

Don't ever give up on your quest to quit. Becoming addiction free is a choice that you have the power to make. Overcoming addiction is not easy, but it is achievable. No one else has control of your choices, unless you give them this control. So if you make this choice following through with action will show that you mean it.

Do you want to stop participating with your habit or substance? Why?

_____

_____

_____

_____

_____

_____

_____

_____

_____

_____

_____

_____

_____

_____

_____

_____

_____

_____

Everyday I am committed to making better choices for myself.

I want you to know, you can heal from addiction.
It is treatable. Don't ever give up on yourself.
If you slip up, just start over.
and over…and over…and over…and over…and over…and over…
It's ok, you will get there.

Addiction Journal

List the reasons your life would be better without your addiction. Make a copy of this list and carry it with you everywhere you go. Every time you get a craving to participate with your habit or substance, read this list.

_____

_____

_____

_____

_____

_____

_____

_____

_____

_____

I love myself enough to make choices that are for my highest good.

What has held you back from committing to stop your habit or substance?

_____

_____

_____

_____

_____

_____

_____

_____

_____

_____

Addiction Inventory

If you are committed to stopping your addiction,
there will be improvement with these 3 addictive symptoms.

Directions: mark the box that most applies.

0=never / 1=hardly ever / 2=sometimes / 3=often / 4=usually

Addictive Symptoms	0	1	2	3	4
Denial: Rationalize and minimize how often I participate with my habits. Dishonest with others. Defensive if confronted.					
Blame: Don't take ownership or responsibility For the way my life is. I make excuses and justify my behavior.					
Life Consequences: Negative outcomes from habits. Loss of job, relationships, money, etc. Lack spiritual connection or inner peace.					

Score 0-3 points Non-addictive personality traits	Score 4-6 points Mild addictive traits	Score 6-9 points Moderate addictive traits (seek treatment).	Score 10-12 points Severe addictive traits (seek treatment).

Was there a difference in your score from page 21, with any of your symptoms?
Which symptoms do you still need more mastery in?

_____

_____

_____

_____

Which symptoms do you see improvement with?

_____

_____

_____

_____

VISUALIZE YOURSELF WITHOUT THE ADDICTION

CHAPTER 7
Effective Strategy #2
Visualize yourself without the addiction.

Close your eyes and practice seeing yourself free of your addiction in situations or places where you have previously participated with your addiction.

For example, if you struggle with alcoholism close your eyes and visualize yourself sober in a situation or place where you usually drink alcohol.

Practice this daily, even if you relapse. Hold the visual of yourself free of the addiction.

In order to manifest sobriety in your 'real life,' you must first see yourself free of the addiction in your imagination.

This can eventually become your reality. We are reprogrammable!

When you visualize yourself without the addiction, how do you feel?

_____

_____

_____

_____

_____

_____

Are there places or situations that are harder for you to visualize yourself sober or free from your habit? Write about this.

_____

_____

_____

_____

_____

_____

Homework

Write down several sobriety affirmations. Put them in all the places that you typically relapse, so that when you see these, it will reinforce your abstinence from your habit or substance. Sample sobriety affirmations are on page 34.

Addiction Inventory

If you are visualizing yourself every day without the addiction,
there will be improvement with these 3 addictive symptoms.

Directions: mark the box that most applies.

0=never / 1=hardly ever / 2=sometimes / 3=often / 4=usually

Addictive Symptoms	0	1	2	3	4
Compulsive: Impulsive thoughts and behaviors. "All or Nothing" thinking. Lack of moderation.					
Blame: Don't take ownership or responsibility For the way my life is. I make excuses and justify my behavior.					
Life Consequences: Negative outcomes from habits. Loss of job, relationships, money, etc. Lack spiritual connection or inner peace.					

Score 0-3 points	Score 4-6 points	Score 6-9 points	Score 10-12 points
Non-addictive personality traits	Mild addictive traits	Moderate addictive traits (seek treatment).	Severe addictive traits (seek treatment).

Was there a difference in your score from page 21, with any of your symptoms?

Which symptoms do you still need more mastery in?

_____

_____

_____

Which symptoms do you see improvement with?

_____

_____

_____

CHAPTER 8

Effective Strategy #3

Delay Giving In To Your Habit

Each time you get a strong craving to participate with your substance or habit say, "I don't do that anymore." Then do something else for a few minutes until the craving decreases.

Examples Of Delay Tactics

- Leave the room you are in.
- Take a walk.
- Focus on a good memory.
- Journal your feelings.
- Draw.
- Call a friend.
- Say sobriety affirmations.
- Listen to a song.
- Be with another human being.
- Create a hobby.
- Read an article.

Remember that strong cravings are short term. They only last from several seconds up to a minute. Each time you give into your craving you are reinforcing the unwanted habit.

Instead, practice going longer and longer amounts of time without giving into your habit by choosing a different response to the craving. Over time giving in to your craving to participate with your habit weakens and your ability to override it becomes do-able! YEAH!

What delay tactics will you practice when you have a strong craving?

_____

_____

_____

_____

_____

_____

_____

_____

_____

_____

_____

_____

_____

_____

_____

_____

_____

Sobriety Affirmations (Affirmations are stating truths in advance)

A sober me is a better me.

Each day I choose to make better choices for myself.

I will not allow my addiction(s) or habit(s) to block me from reaching my goals.

I am capable of handling anything that life brings me, one moment at a time.

I start the healing process from addiction, when I focus on being free from my addiction.

Serving others takes the focus off of me.

Each day I practice more moderation in my life.

I am capable of soothing my emotions instead of medicating them.

As I forgive the past I no longer need to use emotional pain as an excuse to participate with my addiction(s) or habit(s)

I have the power to make healthy choices.

My emotional discomfort can be managed sober, by taking action to resolve my problems.

Addiction Journal

Do you have any thoughts or situations that prompt a strong craving to participate with your habit/compulsion? What are they?

_____

_____

_____

_____

_____

_____

_____

_____

_____

_____

_____

_____

How long have you been able to go without participating in your habit or addiction during thoughts of a craving? Write about this: How did you feel? What did you do?

_____

_____

_____

_____

_____

_____

_____

_____

_____

_____

_____

_____

_____

_____

_____

Escape

Is there something that I can take
That will allow me to escape,
From thoughts of pain
And acts of which I am still to blame?
Is there anything you know of that will work
To blow shame right out of my brain?
Is there a pill I can take,
A cure
That will help to ease all the worry and anxiety,
I endure?
Drugs and alcohol bring such short relief
And the hangover is not worth it to keep.
Do you have a distraction that works?
One that blocks out sorrow and memories that haunt?
Gambling is so expensive,
And pornography is so raunch.
Do you have anything for past hurts and old mistakes?
What prescription do you suggest
Whose side effect is invulnerability to all of life's tests?
How am I supposed to cope with the let downs,
The fears, the unplanned occurrences throughout the day?
How about something for my tormented thoughts that flow?
What about loneliness, do you have a cure?
I tried stuffing down my feelings with loads of food,
But the fat I couldn't endure.
What treatment do you have for loss?
Do you have something that can erase
The feeling of love's cord being cut at its base?
What about the tears—what do you use to hold them back?
Besides the old standby of numbing out with a shot of Jack?
What is the buffer so I no longer have to suffer?
Do you have something I can take that makes me strong
And able to disconnect from rejection?
Continuation with my addictions just causes me dejection.
What relief can you offer that will give me hope,
Without having to turn to my addictions to cope?
What will make me stay sober until this difficult life is over?

— **Elisabeth Davies**

Addiction Journal

Using the poem on the previous page as an example, write your own poem next time you need to distract yourself from giving in to your addiction.

_____
_____
_____
_____
_____
_____
_____
_____

Do you have thoughts or feelings you try to avoid or distract yourself from? What are they?

_____
_____
_____
_____
_____
_____
_____
_____

What thoughts or feelings would you like to have instead?

_____
_____
_____
_____
_____
_____
_____

Addiction Journal

Write about the progress you have noticed with yourself. Have you seen progress with your choices? Do you have more positive thoughts about your recovery? What other areas of your life do you notice progress?

Focusing on the progress you make encourages long-term change.

Addiction Inventory

If you are delaying giving into your habit each time you get a craving,
there will be improvement with these 4 addictive symptoms.

Directions: mark the box that most applies.

0=never / 1=hardly ever / 2=sometimes / 3=often / 4=usually

Addictive symptoms	0	1	2	3	4
Compulsive: Impulsive thoughts and behaviors. 'All or Nothing' thinking. Lack of moderation.					
Low Self-esteem: Self-critical. Allow others to devalue me. Feelings of guilt and shame. Make choices that are not in my best interest.					
Blame: Don't take ownership or responsibility For the way my life is. I make excuses and justify my behavior.					
Life Consequences: Negative outcomes from habits. Loss of job, relationships, money, etc. Lack spiritual connection or inner peace.					

Score 0-4 points	Score 5-8 points	Score 9-12 points	Score 13-16 points
Non-addictive personality traits	Mild addictive traits	Moderate addictive traits (seek treatment)	Severe addictive traits (seek treatment)

Was there a difference in your score from page 21, with any of your symptoms?
Which symptoms do you still need more mastery in?

_____

_____

_____

Which symptoms do you notice improvement with?

_____

_____

_____

HAVE AN ANCHOR

CHAPTER 9
Effective Strategy #4
Have An Anchor

An anchor is something that keeps your mind steady and calm when everything around you feels unstable. An anchor can be a thought you focus on to steady yourself. It can be something physical you carry in your pocket or purse that symbolizes serenity and steadiness. It can be a place you go to that is calm and peaceful. Practice using an anchor every day as a way to steady your thoughts and feelings when they begin feeling out of control.

My Anchor

In the summer of 2001, my husband and I went to Maui, Hawaii. He took a picture of me lying in the water at Seven Sacred Pools. The water felt tantalizing; the warm sun and cool breeze made me feel comfortable and safe. It felt good to be on vacation, with no stress! I remember being totally present for that amazing moment.

When I need an anchor, I look at that picture and breathe in how I felt in that moment. It always steady's my mind again and again.

Samples Of Anchors

- Meditation
- Taking a walk
- Sitting on the beach
- Saying a prayer
- Finding a quiet, calming place
- Listening to soothing music
- Reading a calming book or magazine
- Thinking about a favorite memory
- Keeping your thoughts in the present moment
- Saying comforting affirmations
- Looking at something beautiful

- Holding an object that represents peace
- Breathing out all negative energy from your being

What can you use as an anchor? How does it calm and steady your mind when you focus on it?

_____

_____

_____

_____

_____

_____

_____

_____

_____

_____

What state of mind are you hoping to achieve by participating with your addiction/habit?

_____

_____

_____

_____

_____

_____

_____

_____

_____

_____

How can you achieve this state of mind in a healthier way?

_____

_____

_____

_____

_____

_____

_____

_____

Addiction Inventory

If you are using an anchor each time you feel out of control,
there will be improvement with these 2 addictive symptoms.

Directions: mark the box that most applies.

0=never / 1=hardly ever / 2=sometimes / 3=often / 4=usually

Addictive symptoms	0	1	2	3	4
Compulsive: Impulsive thoughts and behaviors. 'All or Nothing' thinking. Lack of moderation.					
Mood Changes: Irritable. Unpredictable and immature responses Isolative or reclusive.					

Score 0-2 points	Score 3-4 points	Score 5-6 points	Score 7-8 points
Non-addictive personality traits	Mild addictive traits	Moderate addictive traits (seek treatment)	Severe addictive traits (seek treatment)

Was there a difference in your score from page 21, with any of your symptoms?
Which symptoms do you still need more mastery in?

_____

_____

_____

_____

_____

_____

_____

Which symptoms do you notice improvement with?

_____

_____

_____

_____

_____

_____

_____

_____

CHAPTER 10
Effective Strategy #5
Soothe Your Moods And Emotions

Sometimes we use substances or unhealthy habits as a way to soothe our moods and get emotional relief because we haven't acquired healthy skills to tolerate our emotions.

Our thoughts create our moods. If we focus on thoughts that are upsetting to our well-being, it will cause our emotions to become unbalanced. Instead, regulate your emotions with internal thoughts that sooth, encourage, nurture, and uplift you.

Addiction is an external attempt to soothe an internal state.

Examples of self-soothing thoughts

- I am strong enough to handle this situation, one moment at a time.
- I allow myself to become a better problem solver so that I am more equipped to handle all of life's challenges.
- I take deep breaths and slow down so that I can expand my capacity to tolerate uncomfortable feelings.
- My worth is determined by my inherent abilities, not by other people or situational outcomes.
- I forgive my mistakes as a sign that I unconditionally love myself.
- I have more compassion for my situation.
- I have value, whether or not others acknowledge it.
- I can let go of disappointments and learn that everything that happens is to teach me something that will enhance me as a human being.
- As I slow my breathing, my body and mind become more relaxed.

What soothing thoughts can you tell yourself that will help regulate your emotional moods?

_____

_____

_____

_____

Addiction Journal

Is there anything that you participate in that causes a mood change? What about eating, shopping, drugs, alcohol, pornography, gambling, T.V., relationships, work, Internet, video games, etc.?

_____

_____

_____

_____

_____

_____

_____

_____

_____

_____

_____

_____

_____

Write about the mood change you experience.

_____

_____

_____

_____

_____

_____

_____

_____

_____

_____

_____

_____

_____

_____

Addiction Journal

Realistically, what mood do you want to be in each day? What thoughts do you need to focus on to achieve this?

_____

_____

_____

_____

_____

_____

_____

_____

_____

_____

_____

_____

_____

How would achieving this mood impact your participation with your habit or substance?

_____

_____

_____

_____

_____

_____

_____

_____

_____

_____

_____

_____

_____

We must be able to feel good sober, in order to want to stay sober.

Addiction Inventory

If you are choosing thoughts each day that are soothing your moods
and emotions, there will be improvement with these 6 addictive symptoms.

Directions: Mark the box that most applies.

0=never / 1=hardly ever / 2=sometimes / 3=often / 4=usually

Addictive Symptoms	0	1	2	3	4
Compulsive: Impulsive thoughts and behaviors. 'All or Nothing' thinking. Lack of moderation.					
Low Self-esteem: Self-critical. Allow others to devalue me. Feelings of guilt and shame. Make choices that are not in my best interest.					
Blame: Don't take ownership or responsibility for the way my life is. I make excuses and justify my behavior.					
Self-Centered: Inconsiderate of how my words and actions affect others. My wants and needs come first. Undependable					
Mood Changes: Irritable. Unpredictable and immature responses Isolative or reclusive.					
Life Consequences: Negative outcomes from habits. Loss of job, relationships, money, etc. Lack spiritual connection or inner peace.					

Score 0-6 points	Score 7-12 points	Score 13-18 points	Score 19-24 points
Non-addictive personality traits	Mild addictive traits	Moderate addictive traits (seek treatment)	Severe addictive traits (seek treatment)

Was there a difference in your score from page 21, with any of your symptoms?

Which symptoms do you still need more mastery in?

_____

_____

_____

_____

_____

_____

_____

_____

_____

_____

_____

_____

_____

_____

_____

_____

_____

Which symptoms did you notice improvement with?

_____

_____

_____

_____

_____

_____

_____

_____

_____

_____

_____

_____

_____

_____

_____

TAKE CARE OF YOUR BODY

CHAPTER 11
Effective Strategy #6
Take Care Of Your Body

Your body is your vehicle that allows you to physically experience each day in this world.

Taking good care of it by eating healthy, exercising regularly and treating it with value can help it function at its optimal ability.

If we have an addictive personality, we tend to do things to an extreme, by not honoring our body's cues and responses to the way we are treating it.

Examples of negative consequences from not taking care of our body

- Overweight from eating too much food
- Stress and fatigue from working too many hours
- A hangover from drinking too much alcohol
- An injury from exercising or training too hard
- Organ deterioration from using too many drugs
- Sexually transmitted diseases from irresponsible sexual choices
- Respiratory deficits due to smoking too much
- Lack of sleep due to compulsive worrying

A key component to healing addiction is setting limits in what we do.

Physical pain, discomfort or fatigue are a few ways our body lets us know we are surpassing our limits. Next time your body feels fatigued or discomfort, take a short time-out and close your eyes. Ask your body what it needs to reestablish optimal health. Listen to your body's messages. Your body counts on you to give it what it needs.

Some ways to take good care of your body

- Rest when you are tired to de-stress your body.
- Eat foods that are natural and high in nutrients for optimal health.

- Exercise for a minimum of 20 minutes several days a week to keep strong muscles and heart.
- Drink several glasses of water each day to replenish and hydrate.
- Be in nature frequently to restore good energy to your being.
- Play a little bit each day to de-stress and enhance your mood.
- Bathe and groom yourself on a daily basis for hygiene.

Addiction Journal

What do you do when your body feels fatigue or discomfort? Does it help?

What can you do, besides participate with your addiction, to de-stress your body?

Are you good at taking care of your body? What do you do to ensure optimal health?

What would motivate you to become better at physical self-care?

Addiction Inventory

If you are taking good care of your body each day,
there will be improvement with these 5 addictive symptoms.

Directions: Mark the box that most applies.

0=never / 1=hardly ever / 2=sometimes / 3=often / 4=usually

Addictive symptoms	0	1	2	3	4
Compulsive: Impulsive thoughts and behaviors. 'All or Nothing' thinking. Lack of moderation					
Low Self-esteem: Self-critical. Allow others to devalue me. Feelings of guilt and shame. Make choices that are not in my best interest.					
Blame: Don't take ownership or responsibility for the way my life is. I make excuses and justify my behavior.					
Self-Centered: Inconsiderate of how my words and actions affect others. My wants and needs come first. Undependable					
Life Consequences: Negative outcomes from habits. Loss of job, relationships, money, etc. Lack spiritual connection or inner peace.					

Score 0-5 points	Score 6-10 points	Score 11-15 points	Score 16-20 points
Non-addictive personality traits	Mild addictive traits	Moderate addictive traits (seek treatment)	Severe addictive traits (seek treatment)

Was there a difference in your score from page 21, with any of your symptoms?

Which symptoms do you still need more mastery in?

_____

_____

_____

_____

_____

_____

_____

_____

_____

_____

_____

_____

_____

_____

_____

Which symptoms did you notice improvement with?

_____

_____

_____

_____

_____

_____

_____

_____

_____

_____

_____

_____

_____

_____

_____

_____

Strategy 7

Pace yourself

CHAPTER 12
Effective Strategy #7
Pace Yourself!

You don't' have to do it all NOW! If you feel overwhelmed, you probably are NOT pacing yourself. Sometimes we feel we can't get everything done, even if we go at our fastest pace. This can create a lot of stress, and stress can trigger a relapse into an unhealthy habit or addiction.

Skills To Better Pace Yourself

- Focus on doing one thing at a time, instead of two or more. This provides for less stress and fewer mistakes.

- Prioritize what needs to get done today. If there is no negative consequence for not getting it done today, it is not a today priority!

- Focus on goal outcomes and NOT goal time-lines. All goals will be reached as long as we continue to put our time and energy into them. Perseverance produces outcomes!

- If your mind and body feel overwhelmed, stop and take a short time-out. Remove yourself from the stressful situation take a few deep breaths and ask yourself what outcome you are working toward today.

I do life at life's pace.

Life is given to me one moment at a time.

When you get to the very last day of your life, and you look back over everything, what is going to matter?

_____

_____

_____

_____

_____

_____

What you wrote above is what matters today.

Addiction Journal

How good are you at pacing yourself with tasks? Do you pace yourself when you set goals?

If you were to prioritize the most important goal to accomplish today, what is it?

How can you pace yourself with today's goal?

Homework

Write down one problem in your life that you cope with, by using an unhealthy habit or substance. (Example: intimate relationship, family, job. finances, weight, illness, loss/grief etc.)

_____

_____

_____

_____

_____

_____

_____

_____

Each day find one strategy that would help resolve this problem (Example: counseling, learning something new about the problem, changing the way you think/believe about this problem, taking initiative to problem solve, setting boundaries, forgiveness, acceptance, etc.)

_____

_____

_____

_____

_____

_____

_____

_____

Take at least several minutes each day to do one thing that helps resolve this problem. Write down what you did.

_____

_____

_____

_____

_____

_____

_____

_____

Addiction Journal

Write down the progress you see with pacing yourself to resolve this problem.

Addiction Inventory

If you are pacing yourself each day, there will be improvement with these 4 addictive symptoms.

Directions: Mark the box that most applies.

0=never / 1=hardly ever / 2=sometimes / 3=often / 4=usually

Addictive symptoms	0	1	2	3	4
Compulsive: Impulsive thoughts and behaviors. 'All or Nothing' thinking. Lack of moderation.					
Low Self-esteem: Self-critical. Allow others to devalue me. Feelings of guilt and shame. Make choices that are not in my best interest.					
Blame: Don't take ownership or responsibility for the way my life is. I make excuses and justify my behavior.					
Mood Changes: Irritable. Unpredictable and immature responses Isolative or reclusive.					

Score 0-4 points	Score 5-8 points	Score 9-12 points	Score 13-16 points
Non-addictive personality traits	Mild addictive traits	Moderate addictive traits (seek treatment)	Severe addictive traits (seek treatment)

Was there a difference in your score from page 21, with any of your symptoms?
Which symptoms do you still need more mastery in?

_____

_____

_____

_____

Which symptoms do you see improvement with?

_____

_____

_____

_____

SEEK COUNSELING WITH AN ADDICTION SPECIALIST

CHAPTER 13
Effective Strategy #8
Seek Counseling With An Addiction Specialist

Several of my clients, struggling with addiction would tell me they need more life skills, so they don't continue responding in old habitual ways to stress and difficulties. Many of us participate in addictive behavior as a coping mechanism to medicate or distract from the stress in our life. Unresolved situations from our past, also affect our moods and emotions. A trained professional can suggest effective strategies to heal from the past and manage current stressors.

You can heal your past.

Other Ways To Acquire More Skills And Cope, In Addition To Counseling

- Join a support group with others who have struggled with the same addiction as you.

- Forgive everyone who has wronged you, as a way to release past emotional hurts.

- Get an addiction sponsor, mentor, or someone you trust. Share your addictive habits with them, to break the power of denial and allow for help and accountability.

- Interview people who have overcome an addiction. Ask them how they did it and what they found helpful.

- Find a place that grows you spiritually and go there regularly.

- Read addiction books and articles, to gain knowledge about addiction.

- Google 'addiction' on the Internet and go to informative addiction websites.

- Put inspirational quotes and affirmations in all your places of temptation, as a reminder of your commitment to being addiction free.

- Thank God everyday for giving you the strength to be free of addiction.

Addiction Journal

Are you currently working with a counselor or addiction specialist? Why? Why not?

_____

_____

_____

_____

_____

_____

_____

Have you found counseling to be helpful? Why? Why not?

_____

_____

_____

_____

_____

_____

_____

Who have you told about your participation with your substance or habit? Who is your support system? Why have you chosen them for your support system?

_____

_____

_____

_____

_____

_____

Who are you accountable to (besides yourself) for staying addiction free?

_____

_____

_____

_____

_____

_____

Homework

Interview someone who does not struggle with an addiction. Ask them how they manage life's difficulties without participating in addictive habits. Ask what coping skills they use for stress or loss or disappointment. Write down what they told you.

Addiction Inventory

If you are getting counseling with an effective addiction specialist,
there will be improvement with these 6 addictive symptoms.

Directions: Mark the box that most applies.

0=never / 1=hardly ever / 2=sometimes / 3=often / 4=usually

Addictive Symptoms	0	1	2	3	4
Compulsive: Impulsive thoughts and behaviors. 'All or Nothing' thinking. Lack of moderation.					
Denial: Rationalize and minimize how often I participate with my habits. Dishonest with others. Defensive if confronted.					
Low Self-esteem: Self-critical. Allow others to devalue me. Feelings of guilt and shame. Make choices that are not in my best interest.					
Blame: Don't take ownership or responsibility for the way my life is. I make excuses and justify my behavior.					
Self-Centered: Inconsiderate of how my words and actions affect others. My wants and needs come first. Undependable					
Mood Changes: Irritable. Unpredictable and immature responses Isolative or reclusive.					

Score 0-6 points	Score 7-12 points	Score 13-18 points	Score 19-24 points
Non-addictive personality traits	Mild addictive traits	Moderate addictive traits (seek treatment)	Severe addictive traits (seek treatment)

Was there a difference in your score from page 21, with any of your symptoms?
Which symptoms do you still need more mastery in?

_____

_____

_____

_____

_____

_____

_____

_____

_____

_____

_____

_____

_____

_____

What symptoms do you notice improvement with?

_____

_____

_____

_____

_____

_____

_____

_____

_____

_____

_____

_____

_____

_____

_____

Develop an Effective Relapse Plan

CHAPTER 14

Effective Strategy #9

Develop An Effective Relapse Prevention Plan

Review and check off each plan you have followed every day, to manage your progress with your addiction.

Sample Relapse Prevention Plan

My name: _____

Date that I made my relapse plan: _____

Plan 1: Get rid of everything on my property that makes it easy for me to participate with my addiction. This may include drugs, alcohol, paraphernalia, phone numbers of dealers, certain foods, credit cards, pornography, internet sites and television.

NOTE: If you are not ready to get rid of things that make it easy for you to relapse, you may not be ready to give up your addiction yet. You decide.

Plan 2: Make it more difficult to relapse impulsively. Tell people who know I have participated with my substance or habit that I am currently in recovery from my addiction. Tell them how they can support me in a vulnerable or weak moment.

Plan 3: Read one chapter a day from a Twelve Step book, or a book about addiction. Write down one new thing I learned each day about being addiction free.

Plan 4: Go to a 12 Step meeting or sober group or activity at least one day a week, to reinforce recovery and support.

Plan 5: Get a sponsor or trained support person who does not participate with my addiction. Meet or talk weekly. Each meeting, share with them what my 'addiction free' goal is for the following week.

Plan 6: Pray to God everyday and thank Him for total release and healing from my addiction.

Plan 7: Love myself unconditionally. Do not participate with thoughts that degrade me for any mistake, unaccomplished goal, or relapse. Encourage myself. No shame allowed!

Never, NEVER give up on yourself. Know that one day you will master addiction-free living.

CHAPTER 15

What are the Twelve Steps?

1. We admitted we were powerless over _____ (Whatever it is we are addicted to) and that our lives had become unmanageable.

2. We came to believe that a power greater than ourselves could restore us to sanity.

3. We made a decision to turn our will and our lives over to the care of God as we understood him.

4. We made a searching and fearless moral inventory of ourselves.

5. We admitted to God, to ourselves and to another human being the exact nature of our wrongs.

6. We were entirely ready to have God remove all these defects of character.

7. We humbly asked God to remove our shortcomings.

8. We made a list of all the people we had harmed, and became willing to make amends to them all.

9. We made direct amends to such people wherever possible, except when to do so would injure them or others.

10. We continued to take personal inventory and when we were wrong, we promptly admitted it.

11. We sought through prayer and meditation to improve our conscious contact with God as we understood him, praying only for knowledge of his will for us and the power to carry that out.

12. Having had a spiritual awakening as the result of these steps, we tried to carry this message to other addicts and to practice these principles in all our affairs.

The 12 steps are reprinted with permission of Alcoholics Anonymous World Services, Inc. This does not mean that AA has reviewed or approved the contents of this publication, or that they agree with the views expressed herein. AA is a program of recovery from alcoholism only. Use of the 12 steps for programs or activities that address other problems, do not imply otherwise.

What is your Relapse Prevention Plan?

Plan 1

Plan 2

Plan 3

Plan 4

Plan 5

Plan 6

Addiction Journal

Show your relapse plan to your counselor, addiction specialist, sponsor or mentor. Ask for their feedback. What did they say?

Addiction Inventory

If you are following an effective relapse plan, there will be improvement with these 2 addictive symptoms.

Directions: mark the box that most applies.

0=never / 1=hardly ever / 2=sometimes / 3=often / 4=usually

Addictive symptoms	0	1	2	3	4
Blame: Don't take ownership or responsibility for the way my life is. I make excuses and justify my behavior.					
Life Consequences: Negative outcomes from habits. Loss of job, relationships, money, etc. Lack spiritual connection or inner peace.					

Score 0-2 points	Score 3-4 points	Score 5-6 points	Score 7-8 points
Non-addictive personality traits	Mild addictive traits	Moderate addictive traits (seek treatment)	Severe addictive traits (seek treatment)

Was there a difference in your score from page 21, with any of your symptoms?

Which symptoms do you still need more mastery in?

_____

_____

_____

_____

_____

_____

_____

_____

_____

_____

_____

_____

_____

Which symptoms do you notice an improvement with?

SERVE OTHERS INSTEAD OF YOURSELF

CHAPTER 16

Effective Strategy #10

Serve Others Instead Of Yourself

Addiction is a self-serving activity. It is of no benefit to anyone else. Each week pick someone or something to do that serves and benefits someone else. This will help take the focus off of you and allow you to be more valuable to others.

We were NOT put on this planet to be self-serving. We were put here to serve others with our inherent talents and abilities.

Examples of some inherent talents and abilities.
Do some of these describe you?

- Intelligent

- Creative

- Ingenious

- Artistic

- Helpful

- Musically inclined

- Loving

- Patient

- Empathetic

- Communicative

- Athletic

- Witty

- Intuitive

- Wise

- Discerning

- Encouraging

Some people are natural…

- Teachers
- Leaders
- Healers
- Fixers
- Writers
- Promoters
- Thinkers
- Builders

Nobody or nothing can strip away your inherent talents and abilities.

They are a part of your core personality.

Allow them full expression for an authentic you!

Addiction Journal

What talents and abilities do you have that can be of service to another person?

_____

_____

_____

_____

_____

_____

_____

Who can you serve with your talents and abilities this week? What will you do?

_____

_____

_____

_____

_____

_____

_____

_____

How can this benefit them?

_____

_____

_____

_____

_____

_____

_____

_____

Each one should use whatever gift he has received to serve others

1 Peter 4:10

Homework

Pick one person each day that you can serve in some way, with your inherent talents and abilities. Write about their response and what impact it had on you.

Day 1

_____

_____

_____

_____

_____

_____

_____

_____

Day 2

_____

_____

_____

_____

_____

_____

_____

_____

Day 3

_____

_____

_____

_____

_____

_____

_____

_____

Day 4

Day 5

Day 6

Addiction Journal

What effect does serving others have on your self-serving desires to participate in unhealthy habits and substances?

_____

_____

_____

_____

_____

_____

_____

_____

_____

_____

_____

_____

_____

_____

_____

_____

_____

_____

_____

_____

_____

_____

_____

_____

_____

_____

_____

Never allow your addiction to stop you from doing what you were created to do.
You offer value to others when you are serving with your talents and abilities.

Addiction Inventory

If you are serving others instead of yourself, there will be improvement with these 2 addictive symptoms.

Directions: mark the box that most applies.

0=never / 1=hardly ever / 2=sometimes / 3=often / 4=usually

Addictive symptoms	0	1	2	3	4
Low Self-esteem: Self-critical. Allow others to devalue me. Feelings of guilt and shame. Make choices that are not in my best interest.					
Self-Centered: Inconsiderate of how my words and actions affect others. My wants and needs come first. Undependable					

Score 0-2 points Non-addictive personality traits	**Score 3-4 points** Mild addictive traits	**Score 5-6 points** Moderate addictive traits (seek treatment)	**Score 7-8 points** Severe addictive traits (seek treatment)

Was there a difference in your score from page 21, with any of your symptoms?

Which symptoms do you still need more mastery in?

_____

_____

_____

_____

_____

_____

Which symptoms did you notice improvement with?

_____

_____

_____

_____

_____

_____

_____

Strategy 11

keep your thoughts in the now

CHAPTER 17

Effective Strategy #11

Keep Your Thoughts In The Now

Do not allow your mind to jump to the future, or ruminate on the past. Always be conscious of keeping your mind where your body is. "…addiction occurs in an area of the brain called the mesolimbic dopamine system that is not under conscious control."(14) We can become unconscious of our addiction when we allow ourselves to disconnect, or not be fully conscious of our choice in the present moment.

One way to become conscious or connected to the present moment is through the conscious awareness exercise.

Conscious Awareness Exercise

Close your eyes and focus your entire attention on how your body breathes all by itself. Do not assist your body in any way at all. Keep your eyes closed until your body has taken three complete inhalation/exhalation breaths on its own. Now open your eyes and focus your entire attention on your current surroundings. What colors are around you? What objects are around you? What sounds do you hear? What's the temperature? Is anything moving or still? Are there any smells, you are aware of? Answer each of these questions, one at a time, until your mind becomes fully present in this current moment.

This exercise takes only a minute or two. Do this brief exercise each time you have a craving or impulse to participate in your addictive habit. With continued practice, you'll eventually be able to do the conscious awareness exercise with your eyes open.

When you keep your thoughts in the now, you are in control of what you are giving yourself permission to acknowledge and participate with. Giving into your craving and participating in your addiction or habit, allows you to disconnect from your surroundings and allows for denial of impact and repercussions that come from participating with your addiction or habit.

Now is now. Are you going to be here or not?

Addiction Journal

How often do you keep your thoughts in the now, aware of each decision and choice that you make?

_____

_____

_____

_____

_____

_____

_____

Where is your body right now? Is your mind fully focused on your body right now? What is your body touching?

_____

_____

_____

_____

_____

_____

_____

Find your pulse by putting your hand on your heart, wrist or neck. Now take a slow, deep breath. Slowly count to four. Exhale, counting slowly to four. What did you notice about this experience? While you were doing this exercise, were you thinking about anything else, or were you focused on the present task at hand?

_____

_____

_____

_____

_____

_____

_____

Addiction Inventory

If you are keeping your thoughts in the now, there will be improvement with these 4 addictive symptoms.

Directions: Mark the box that most applies.

0=never / 1=hardly ever / 2=sometimes / 3=often / 4=usually

Addictive symptoms	0	1	2	3	4
Compulsive: Impulsive thoughts and behaviors. 'All or Nothing' thinking. Lack of moderation.					
Blame: Don't take ownership or responsibility for the way my life is. I make excuses and justify my behavior.					
Mood Changes: ** Irritable. Unpredictable and immature responses Isolative or reclusive.					
Life Consequences: Negative outcomes from habits. Loss of job, relationships, money, etc. Lack spiritual connection or inner peace.					

Score 0-4 points	Score 5-8 points	Score 9-12 points	Score 13-16 points
Non-addictive personality traits	Mild addictive traits	Moderate addictive traits (seek treatment)	Severe addictive traits (seek treatment)

Was there a difference in your score from page 21, with any of your symptoms?

Which symptoms do you still need more mastery in?

_____

_____

_____

What symptoms did you notice improvement with?

_____

_____

_____

** Staying in the now helps with mood changes specifically caused by anxiety (restlessness, feeling keyed up or on edge, fatigue, irritability, muscle tension, difficulty concentrating and sleep disturbances).

Believe in Yourself

it's so hard
to believe
in myself
sometimes

CHAPTER 18

Effective Strategy #12

Believe In Yourself

If you have good self-esteem and a loving relationship with yourself, you will make less self-destructive choices. Low self-esteem is a core problem that fuels addiction. We become vulnerable to medicate or distract from thoughts that are harsh, critical and unloving. They disallow wellbeing and can lead to mood imbalance. Make a commitment to refuse to participate with thoughts of self-doubt. This will allow you to move through life's obstacles easier.

Even if nobody else believes in you, it is your responsibility to believe in you. You are the only one who is in control of how you treat yourself. Never give up on yourself or abandon yourself, emotionally. Be your best encourager and supporter, regardless of what life presents to you.

If life knocks you down 10 times, get up 11 times.

Some ways to believe in yourself and build good self-esteem

- Make a list of things you are good at and like about yourself. Read this list daily and add to it weekly, to remind yourself of your worth.

- Tell yourself that you forgive yourself for ALL past mistakes. Mistakes are opportunities to recognize areas needing more mastery.

- Do not criticize yourself with your thoughts. This is NOT a problem solving technique! Instead, be gentle on yourself and focus on finding solutions to improve.

- Focus on affirming who you want to be and how you want to behave, rather than ruminating about your setbacks. This encourages you being successful.

- Do mirror work. Look yourself in the eyes each day and tell yourself, "I am here to support you through life. I am on your team!"

- Never allow a person or situation to determine your worth. Your worth is determined by your inherent gifts that you were born with.

- Encourage yourself when you go through difficult times. Visualize yourself becoming stronger and more capable of enduring life's challenges.

- Do good self-care. Honor your mind and body by giving yourself what you need for optimal health.

- Stand up for yourself when others put you down. Set boundaries with people regarding what you need from them.

I am good enough just as I am.

Addiction Journal

What are some things you like about yourself?

_____

_____

_____

_____

_____

_____

_____

_____

What are some things you do well?

_____

_____

_____

_____

_____

_____

_____

_____

Have you forgiven yourself for all past mistakes? How does this impact the way you feel about yourself?

_____

_____

_____

_____

_____

_____

_____

Are you critical of yourself for certain things? Which things?

_____
_____
_____
_____
_____
_____
_____

What would be a more loving way to think about your imperfections?

_____
_____
_____
_____
_____
_____
_____

Have you allowed other people or situations to affect your self-esteem? Who?

_____
_____
_____
_____
_____
_____
_____

How can you become the only one who determines this?

_____
_____
_____
_____
_____
_____

Self-esteem comes from self, not others.

Homework

Every day get in front of a mirror. Look yourself directly in the eyes. Say, "I love you _____ [your name]_____. I am sorry for things I have said or done in the past that have not helped you. Each day I will make better choices, so you know you are loved."

Write down thoughts that come up while you are doing this exercise. Notice your thoughts changing as you continue to penetrate the core of your being with this loving message.

1st day my thoughts were…

_____

_____

_____

2nd day my thoughts were…

_____

_____

_____

3rd day my thoughts were…

_____

_____

_____

4th day my thoughts were…

_____

_____

_____

5th day my thoughts were…

_____

_____

_____

6th day my thoughts were…

_____

_____

_____

Addiction Inventory

If you believe in yourself each day, there will be improvement with these 3 addictive symptoms.

Directions: mark the box that most applies.

0=never / 1=hardly ever / 2=sometimes / 3=often / 4=usually

Addictive Symptoms	0	1	2	3	4
Low Self-esteem: Self-critical. Allow others to devalue me. Feelings of guilt and shame. Make choices that are not in my best interest.					
Blame: Don't take ownership or responsibility For the way my life is. I make excuses and justify my behavior.					
Mood Changes: Irritable. Unpredictable and immature responses. Isolative or reclusive.					

Score 0-3 points	Score 4-6 points	Score 6-9 points	Score 10-12 points
Non-addictive personality traits	Mild addictive traits	Moderate addictive traits (seek treatment).	Severe addictive traits (seek treatment).

Was there a difference in your score from page 21, with any of your symptoms?

Which symptoms do you still need more mastery in?

_____

_____

_____

_____

_____

Which symptoms do you see improvement with?

_____

_____

_____

_____

_____

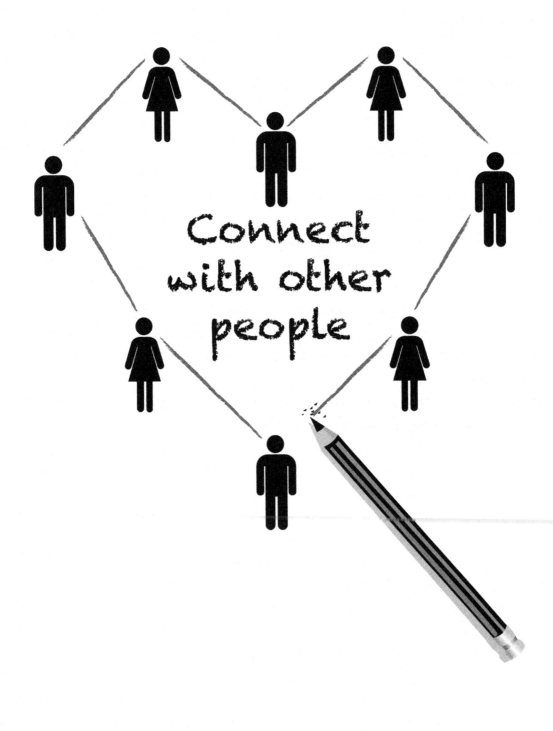

Connect with other people

CHAPTER 19

Effective Strategy #13

Connect With Other People

Keep your heart open to others. Don't put walls up that prevent you from appreciating or connecting with other people. Often times we participate with our substance or habit as a way to hide our vulnerabilities and stay disconnected from others. We may feel that one way to protect ourselves from rejection, hurt or abandonment is by not letting others get close to us.

Forgiveness is what heals old hurts, not walls.

Having a healthy connected relationship means the relationship is mutually beneficial. Both people have the other person's best interest in mind. Contributing to other people's lives in a meaningful way indicates that we are NOT self-centered.

Having healthy, connected relationships helps us manage our addiction, by gaining insight and growing from the input, love, wisdom and accountability from others. These relationships increase our chances of building a multidimensional and dynamic support system.

Having a loving accepting relationship with our self helps us persevere through the emotional risks that are involved when we connect with others.

Some Ways To Connect With Others

- Initiate conversations with other people. Do not wait for them to start.

- Look for something good in every person. This will help you like people.

- Do not judge others. Judgment prevents connection.

- Remain open and unguarded so people can connect with you.

- Learn about other people. Find out something they like or are interested in and share what you know with them.

- Practice sharing vulnerable information with people who love you. Vulnerability is necessary for deep connection with others.

- Be present and attentive with people. This invites them to connect with you.

- Maintain eye contact and smile. Others will sense you are open to connecting.

- Stay in contact with people. This lets them know you are interested in staying connected.

People must be taken as they are, and we should never try to
make them or ourselves better by quarreling with them.

—Edmund Burke

Addiction Journal

Do you allow for connection in your relationships? Which relationships?

_____

_____

_____

_____

_____

_____

_____

_____

_____

_____

_____

_____

_____

_____

Write about a relationship where you felt connected and ended up being hurt.

Did this change the way you connected in future relationships? Why?

_____

_____

_____

_____

_____

_____

_____

_____

_____

_____

_____

Do you share your vulnerabilities with others? Which ones? How have these interactions gone?

Do you try to hide any of your vulnerabilities from others? Which ones? Why?

What vulnerability(s) are you most afraid to let others see? Why?

Homework

Pick one person who loves you whom you have walls up with. Practice one of the nine ways to connect (Page 95 under Some Ways To Connect With Others) each day until you have practiced all nine connecting strategies with this person.

How did these connecting strategies impact your connection with your loved one? Were there any strategies that were more difficult to practice? Which ones?

Addiction Inventory

If you are connecting with other human beings each day,
there will be improvement with these 2 addictive symptoms.

Directions: mark the box that most applies.

0=never / 1=hardly ever / 2=sometimes / 3=often / 4=usually

Addictive symptoms	0	1	2	3	4
Self-Centered: Inconsiderate of how my words and actions affect others. My wants and needs come first. Undependable					
Mood Changes: Irritable. Unpredictable and immature responses. Isolative or reclusive.					

Score 0-2 points	Score 3-4 points	Score 5-6 points	Score 7-8 points
Non-addictive personality traits	Mild addictive traits	Moderate addictive traits (seek treatment)	Severe addictive traits (seek treatment)

Was there a difference in your score from page 21, with any of your symptoms?

Which symptoms do you still need more mastery in?

_____

_____

_____

_____

_____

Which symptoms do you see improvement with?

_____

_____

_____

_____

_____

SACRIFICE YOUR ADDICTION

CHAPTER 20

Effective Strategy #14

Sacrifice Your Addiction

Sacrificing your addiction means doing an action that demonstrates your addiction no longer has power over you.

Go to a place in nature. Find a large rock, or make an altar from flat rocks.

Put whatever it is you are addicted to (alcohol, drugs, food, credit card spending, cigarettes, video games, pornography tapes, T.V. etc.) on top of the altar. If you are addicted to work, you can use something that symbolizes work. If you are addicted to a relationship, use a picture of the person or something of theirs that represents them. If the item(s) can be burned, burn it on the altar. If the item(s) cannot be burned, or it's illegal to start a fire where you are, leave it on the altar if it is safe to do so.

Once your item of addiction is on the altar, it can help to say a prayer or affirm what you intend to happen following the sacrifice.

Sample Sacrifice Affirmation

As I leave my addiction here today, I move forward to a life free of _____
_____ addiction

Sample Sacrifice Prayer

"Dear God, today I am asking you to take my addiction from me I sacrifice it to you and release it from my life. Things that seem impossible for me are not impossible for you.

I leave my addiction on this alter today, which symbolizes me leaving my addiction behind to take steps toward a life that is free of unhealthy dependency. I thank you in advance for taking this addiction from me. Amen. It is done."

Walk Away And Leave Your Addiction On The Altar.

Therefore I tell you, whatever you ask for in prayer,
believe that you have received it, and it will be yours. **Words of Jesus,**

Mark: 11:24

Addiction Journal

Do you have any fears that arise when you consider giving up your addiction/ habit? What are they?

_____

_____

_____

_____

_____

_____

_____

_____

_____

_____

_____

_____

Do you feel you will lose a part of yourself or your lifestyle if you give up your addiction/ habit? What parts?

_____

_____

_____

_____

_____

_____

_____

_____

_____

_____

_____

_____

What addiction are you ready to sacrifice? Pick one. Once you master freedom from one addiction, you can do this exercise with the next one.

_____
_____
_____
_____
_____
_____
_____
_____
_____
_____
_____
_____
_____
_____
_____

Write about your sacrifice experience.

_____
_____
_____
_____
_____
_____
_____
_____
_____
_____
_____
_____
_____
_____
_____

You can sacrifice an addiction more than once to reinforce the letting go process.

Is it hard for you to sacrifice things in your life, even if you know they are not for your highest good? Why?

I let go of all the things in my life that are not for my highest good,
so that I am in alignment with my true purpose; a life of hope and a successful future.

Addiction Inventory

If you sacrifice your addiction, there will be improvement with these 3 addictive symptoms.

Directions: mark the box that most applies.

0=never / 1=hardly ever / 2=sometimes / 3=often / 4=usually

Addictive Symptoms	0	1	2	3	4
Denial: Rationalize and minimize how often I participate with my habits. Dishonest with others. Defensive if confronted.					
Blame: Don't take ownership or responsibility For the way my life is. I make excuses and justify my behavior.					
Life Consequences: Negative outcomes from habits. Loss of job, relationships, money, etc. Lack spiritual connection or inner peace.					

Score 0-3 points	Score 4-6 points	Score 6-9 points	Score 10-12 points
Non-addictive personality traits	Mild addictive traits	Moderate addictive traits (seek treatment).	Severe addictive traits (seek treatment).

Was there a difference in your score from page 21, with any of your symptoms?

Which symptoms do you still need more mastery in?

_____

_____

_____

_____

_____

Which symptoms do you notice an improvement with?

_____

_____

_____

_____

_____

STRENGTHEN YOUR INTERNAL BOUNDARIES

CHAPTER 21

Effective Strategy #15

Strengthen Your Internal Boundaries To Contain Uncomfortable Feelings

A boundary is a limit we set with our self and others. If we were raised in an environment where our boundaries were not respected, we will have damaged boundaries, when it comes to respecting ourselves. Strong boundaries are necessary for managing an addiction, because they allow us to set limits with how much and how often we participate with unhealthy habits and substances.

Examples of damaged boundaries

- Failing to keep promises we make to ourselves about limiting our intake of food, alcohol or drugs.

- Failing to keep promises regarding our behavior to **others or ourselves**.

- Failing to follow through with goals we set for ourselves.

- Allowing others to mistreat us.

- Not following through with our responsibilities.

As addicts, we tend to rely on the limits and boundaries others set with us as our cue that our behavior has crossed the line. We override our own internal boundary, to get our way even if 'our way' is not in our best interest.

We can relearn how to set healthy boundaries with ourselves.

Take a minute or two each day to ask yourself, "What is one choice I can make today that is in my best interest?" Write down your answer and keep it somewhere where you can see it all day. When you get a strong urge to override what is in your best interest, take in a very deep breath, till you cannot hold any more oxygen. Visualize yourself expanding your space to contain that uncomfortable feeling of not getting your way. Say to your self, "Just for this moment, I am strengthening my boundary by doing what is in my best interest." Breathe out and steady yourself in the right choice.

One choice that I can make today that is in my best interest is...

_____

_____

_____

What uncomfortable feelings arise when you do not get your way?

_____

_____

_____

_____

_____

What results have happened to you from not setting healthy internal boundaries?

_____

_____

_____

_____

_____

_____

_____

_____

_____

_____

_____

Some results of not setting healthy boundaries

- Someone who knows us tells us because of our addiction or habit it is too difficult to stay in a relationship with us.

- We have difficulty keeping a good job due to our addiction(s) or compulsive behavior.

- We have financial set backs, bad credit and money problems due to our addiction or impulsive spending habits.

- We lack physical health and have low energy, due to our addiction(s) or unhealthy habit(s).

- We have legal problems due to our addiction(s) or compulsive behavior.

- We lack inner peace or a sense of spirituality due to our addiction(s) or self-defeating habit(s).

- We lack purpose, fulfillment or meaning in our life by using our addiction(s) or compulsive habit(s) to distract or delay taking action toward our goals.

Addiction Journal

What addiction(s) or compulsive habit(s) do you not set boundaries with, even though you know it is not in your best interest?

_____

_____

_____

_____

_____

_____

_____

_____

_____

_____

_____

_____

_____

What addiction or compulsive habit are you willing to set a boundary for today? How can you hold strong and honor your boundary?

_____

_____

_____

_____

_____

_____

_____

_____

_____

_____

_____

_____

Addiction Journal

Were your boundaries disrespected through abuse (verbal, physical, sexual) or neglect growing up? How has this affected the boundaries you set with yourself or others?

_____
_____
_____
_____
_____
_____
_____
_____
_____
_____
_____
_____
_____
_____
_____
_____

What choices do you make that disrespect your boundaries?

_____
_____
_____
_____
_____
_____
_____
_____
_____
_____
_____
_____
_____
_____
_____

Addiction Inventory

If you are strengthening your internal boundaries every day,
there will be improvement with these 6 addictive symptoms.

Directions: Mark the box that most applies.

0=never / 1=hardly ever / 2=sometimes / 3=often / 4=usually

Addictive symptoms	0	1	2	3	4
Compulsive: Impulsive thoughts and behaviors. 'All or Nothing' thinking. Lack of moderation.					
Denial: Rationalize and minimize how often I participate with my habits . Dishonest with others, Defensive if confronted.					
Low Self-esteem: Self-critical. Allow others to devalue me. Feelings of guilt and shame. Make choices that are not in my best interest					
Blame: Don't take ownership or responsibility For the way my life is. I make excuses and justify my behavior.					
Self-Centered: Inconsiderate of how my words and actions affect others. My wants and needs come first. Undependable					
Life Consequences: Negative outcomes from habits. Loss of job, relationships, money, etc. Lack spiritual connection or inner peace.					

Score 0-6 points	Score 7-12 points	Score 13-18 points	Score 19-24 points
Non-addictive personality traits	Mild addictive traits	Moderate addictive traits (seek treatment)	Severe addictive traits (seek treatment)

Was there a difference in your score from page 21, with any of your symptoms?

Which symptoms do you still need more mastery in?

_____

_____

_____

_____

Which symptoms do you notice an improvement with?

_____
_____
_____
_____
_____
_____
_____
_____
_____
_____
_____
_____
_____
_____
_____

What kind of a life can you create, that would make you want to stay addiction free?

_____
_____
_____
_____
_____
_____
_____
_____
_____
_____
_____
_____
_____
_____

You can make your dreams come true.

Addiction Journal

Some things I have learned about myself by participating in addiction and compulsive habits are...

Some things that I have done that I am proud of, regardless of my participation with addiction and compulsive habits are...

Addiction Journal

Some specific things that I think will be effective in keeping me free from my addiction(s) and compulsive habit(s) are …

_____

_____

_____

_____

_____

_____

_____

_____

_____

_____

_____

_____

_____

_____

_____

_____

_____

_____

_____

_____

_____

_____

_____

_____

I can be free of habits that are not healthy for me.

Regardless of the lie they convincingly try to feed me.

My life can be good!

I can learn to live addiction free and have a life

Where I allow love to be continually expressed through me.

Just for today, I will help myself start healing from my addiction by...

About the Author

Elisabeth Davies, MC has been a counselor since 1989. She holds a masters degree in counseling and is the founder of Bright Alternatives Inc. (www.brightalternatives.com). She is the creator and author of Good Things Emotional Healing workbooks, cards and other products. For exciting downloads or to participate in interactive journaling, please visit www.goodthingsemotionalhealing.com.

About the Illustrator

Bryan Marshall currently resides in Yukon Territory, Canada. He has been freelancing as an illustrator and graphic designer since 2001. Bryan is originally from Vancouver, British Columbia, where he studied fine arts at Emily Carr Institute of Art and Design and animation at the Art Institute of Vancouver.

Bryan can be contacted through his website at www.bmar13.com.

Look for these other

Good Things Emotional Healing Journals

COMING SOON

Good Things, Emotional Healing Journal—Anger

Good Things, Emotional Healing Journal—Anxiety

Good Things, Emotional Healing Journal—Body Image

Good Things, Emotional Healing Journal—Dependency

Good Things, Emotional Healing Journal—Depression

Good Things, Emotional Healing Journal—Guilt

Good Things, Emotional Healing Journal—Happiness

Good Things, Emotional Healing Journal—Loss

Good Things, Emotional Healing Journal—Love

Good Things, Emotional Healing Journal—Peace

Good Things, Emotional Healing Journal—Relationships

Good Things, Emotional Healing Journal—Self-Esteem

Good Things, Emotional Healing Journal—Stress

Good Things, Emotional Healing Journal—Trust

Good Things, Emotional Healing Journal—Truth

Stories from the Couch

Appendix

(1) "Addiction" www.stopaddiction.com/index.php/addiction

(2) "Obesity and Overweight" www.cdc.gov/nchs/fastats/overwt.htm

(3) "BJ Gallagher: Is President Obama Addicted to Nicotine?" www.tobacco.org/news/297859.html

(4) "Almost One in 10 Americans Has Addiction Disorder" www.jointogether.org/news/research/summaries/2004/almost-one-in-10-americans.html

(5) "NIDA InfoFacts: Marijuana" www.nida.nih.gov/infofacts/marijuana.html

(6) "The 40-Hour Work Week- Dead or Alive" www.homepages.indiana.edu/040904/text/workweek.shtml

(7) "Credit Card Debt: The Average Americans Debt. Fraud, Credit Companies" www.associatedcontent.com/article/1303282/credit_card_debt_the_average_americ ans.htm?cat=3

(8) "Kids Spend Nearly 55 Hours a Week Watching T.V., Texting, Playing Video Games..." www.thedailygreen.com/environmental-news/latest/kids-television-47102701

(9) "The Disease of Addiction" www.articlesbase.com/self-improvement-articles/the-disease-of-addiction-824981.html

(10) " Big Mystery: What Causes Addiction? www.msnbc.com/id/3076712

(11) "What Is Chemical Imbalance?" www.wisegeek.com/what-is-a-chemical-imbalance.htm

(12) "The Genetics of Addiction" www.addictionsandrecovery.org/is-addiction-a-disease.htm

(13) "Substance Abuse and Mental Health" www.helpguide.org/mental/dual_diagnosis.htm

(14) Susan Froemke and John Hoffman, Addiction Why Can't They Just Stop? New York: Rodale Inc., 2007. Page 37.

Resources

Alcoholics Anonymous (AA) www.alcoholics-anonymous.org (212) 870-3400

Center for Substance Abuse Prevention (301) 443-0365

Computer/video game addiction www.computergamingaddiction.com 1 (888)-452-1869

Free Addiction Helpline www.freeaddictionhelpline.com (866)-569-7077

Gamblers Anonymous. (213)-386-8789

Love Addiction www.loveaddiction.com. 1 (888) 987-6129

Narcotics Anonymous. www.na.org. (818)-997-3822

Nicotine addiction. www.cigarrest.com 1-(800)-338-0631

Overeaters Anonymous. www.oa.org. (505)-891-2664

Sex addicts anonymous. www.sexaa.org. 1 (800)-477-8191

Shopping Addiction. www.stoppingovershoping.com

SMART Recovery. www.smartrecovery.org. (866)-951-5357.

References

Books

Edward Khantzian, Kurt Halliday and William McAuliffe, *Addiction and the Vulnerable Self*. New York: The Guilford Press, 1990.

Katherine Eban, Katherine Ketcham, David Sheff and Larkin Warren. *Addiction Why Can't They Just Stop?* New York: Rodale Inc., 2008.

College Dictionary. New York: Random House, 2002.

Alcoholics Anonymous World Services, Inc. *Twelve Steps and Twelve Traditions*. New York: Forty-first Printing, 2005.

Websites

"American Medical Association," last modified 2011, www.ama-assn.org

"Right Health," last modified 2011, www.righthealth.com

"Vault Career Intelligence," last modified 2010, www.vault.com

"Big Mystery: What Causes Addiction?" last modified 2011, http://www.msnbc.msn.com/id/3076712/

"Wise Geek," last modified 2011, www.wisegeek.com/what-is-a-chemical-imbalance.htm

"BJ Gallagher: Is President Obama Addicted to Nicotine?" last modified 2011, www.tobacco.org/news/297859.html

"The Genetics of Addiction," last modified Jan. 24, 2011, http://addictionsandrecovery.org/is-addiction-a-disease.htm

"Substance Abuse and Mental Health," last modified 2010, http://www.helpguide.org/mental/dual_diagnosis.htm

BUY A SHARE OF THE FUTURE IN YOUR COMMUNITY

These certificates make great holiday, graduation and birthday gifts that can be personalized with the recipient's name. The cost of one S.H.A.R.E. or one square foot is $54.17. The personalized certificate is suitable for framing and will state the number of shares purchased and the amount of each share, as well as the recipient's name. The home that you participate in "building" will last for many years and will continue to grow in value.

Here is a sample SHARE certificate:

YES, I WOULD LIKE TO HELP!

*I support the work that Habitat for Humanity does and I want to be part of the excitement! As a donor, I will receive periodic updates on your construction activities but, more importantly, I know my gift will help a family in our community realize the dream of homeownership. **I would like to SHARE in your efforts against substandard housing in my community!*** (Please print below)

PLEASE SEND ME _____ SHARES at $54.17 EACH = $ $_____

In Honor Of: _____

Occasion: (Circle One)   HOLIDAY   BIRTHDAY   ANNIVERSARY

       OTHER: _____

Address of Recipient: _____

Gift From: _____ *Donor Address:* _____

Donor Email: _____

I AM ENCLOSING A CHECK FOR $ $_____ PAYABLE TO HABITAT FOR HUMANITY <u>OR</u> PLEASE CHARGE MY VISA OR MASTERCARD *(CIRCLE ONE)*

Card Number _____ Expiration Date: _____

Name as it appears on Credit Card _____ Charge Amount $ _____

Signature _____

Billing Address _____

Telephone # Day _____ Eve _____

PLEASE NOTE: Your contribution is tax-deductible to the fullest extent allowed by law.
Habitat for Humanity • P.O. Box 1443 • Newport News, VA 23601 • 757-596-5553
www.HelpHabitatforHumanity.org

CPSIA information can be obtained at www.ICGtesting.com
Printed in the USA
BVOW09s2353130716

455451BV00022B/455/P